D0459121

SOCCER WORLD
MEXICO

Explore the World Through Soccer

Ethan Zohn & David Rosenberg

Illustrated by Shawn Braley

ACKNOWLEDGMENTS

Ethan would like to dedicate this book to his father, Aaron, who always told him to shoot for the stars; Jenna Morasca for all her love and support; his loving family Rochelle, Lenard, Lee, Delphine, Heidi, Ava, Adin, Oliver, and Isaiah; Paola Peacock-Freidrich; Julian Portilla; and the selfless staff and volunteers of Grassroot Soccer.

David thanks Alex O'Loughlin, Kate Boutilier, Peter Facinelli, and Luca Bella Facinelli for small acts of kindness that made a huge difference; Mitchell Hurwitz, who was the first to ask; Ret. Marine Casey Owens; Kati Pressman and Howard Rosenberg; and Ricardo Dadoo, Arnold Ricalde, and Carolina Lukac for sharing their country. Humble gratitude to Brett Weitzel, Tommy Thompson, Ma Jaya, and Ross McCall for making a difficult journey easier. This book is dedicated to my wife Suzanne Kent for her love; to Ethan for his remarkable spirit; and finally to Paul and Hyla Rosenberg, who started the circle.

This book was manufactured by Transcontinental, Interglobe
Beauceville Québec, Canada
February 2010, Job #49054
ISBN: 978-1-9346705-5-2

Illustrations by Shawn Braley
Questions regarding the ordering of this book should be addressed to
Independent Publishers Group
814 N. Franklin St.
Chicago, IL 60610
www.ipgbook.com

Nomad Press
2456 Christian St.
White River Junction, VT 05001
www.nomadpress.net

INTRODUCTION
Meet Ethan
1

MEET ETHAN

WHO'S READY FOR AN EXCITING ADVENTURE?

My name is Ethan Zohn and I have loved soccer since I was 6 years old. As a professional player I have played all over the world. My favorite matches were in Zimbabwe, Chile, Israel, and Hawaii, just to name a few.

occer is played in almost every nation, so this game is like a common language that brings people together. I can just show up at a field with a ball and instantly make 20 cool new friends.

How would you like to come with me on my *Soccer World* adventures? We will meet young people just like you. They will share their customs and culture with us, like what they eat for breakfast and how to say hello in their language.

"Soccer is called football in other countries."

We'll learn about some special places and even what kinds of animals live in their countries. Along the way, we'll discover fun activities that you can do in your classroom or at home.

So what are you waiting for? Grab your soccer ball and cleats and let's head out on our journey!

VISIT ME!

Because you are my travel buddy, you can go to my website. See photos of the places we visit and find more activities and projects at www.soccerworldadventure.com.

THE NEIGHBOR NATION

Join me on a bus to Mexico for our next *Soccer World* adventure. As we head for Mexico City in the south, I am happy to have some time to get used to the altitude. Mexico City lies 7,349 feet above sea level. The higher you are, the more tired you may feel. While we ride, I can fill you in on the amazing adventure that awaits us.

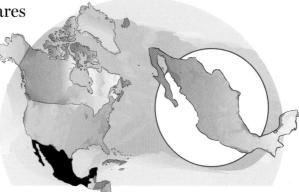

Even though the United States shares a **border** with Mexico, I bet there are many things that would surprise you about our neighbor. Do you know that Mexico has 31 different states and four different coastal areas?

"Many of the foods you eat every day were discovered in Mexico, including my favorite: chocolate!"

WORDS 2 KNOW

altitude: height above sea level.

border: the place where one country meets another.

culture: a way of life of a group of people.

Mexico was home to two important groups of people in history: The Maya and the Aztecs. Their ancient cities were centers of learning and **culture**.

The Maya and Aztec people made huge discoveries in math and science. We still use their ancient discoveries today! Does your birthdate have a zero in it? The Maya were among the first to use a zero in their number system.

WORDS 2 KNOW

astronomy: the study of the stars and planets.

eclipse: when the moon moves between the sun and the earth, blocking the sun's light.

consequence: a result of something happening.

environment: the natural world around us including plants, animals, and air.

pollution: waste that harms the environment.

conqueror: winner in a war.

influence: have an effect on someone or something.

Christianity: a religion whose followers believe in Jesus Christ.

Have you ever gazed at the night sky? The Maya worked out an **astronomy** system without telescopes. They were even able to predict **eclipses**! The next time you visit a movie theater, thank the Aztecs for the popcorn you are eating!

So now you can see how the past really changes the present. That is why knowing history is so important. Everything has a reaction or **consequence**. For example, electricity was an amazing discovery. But using too much of it can harm the **environment**.

Like many modern countries, Mexico is struggling with problems like **pollution** and overcrowding. We will see how Mexico is trying to solve its challenges.

ANCIENT CIVILIZATIONS

The Mayan Civilization was most powerful between 200 BCE and 1000 CE. The Aztec Civilization was at its height between the 1300s and 1500s CE.
BCE stands for Before Common Era. It is a countdown to 0, the year Jesus Christ was born. CE stands for Common Era. It counts up from 0 to the present year.

In our South African adventure, we visited a country that is made up of many different groups of people and nationalities, just like the United States. Mexico is not quite like that. The people of Mexico are the descendents of native Mexican Indians and European **conquerors**, called Mestizos.

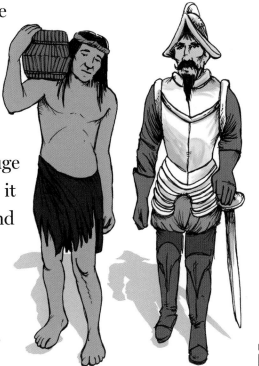

Because Mexico was invaded by Spain beginning in the 1500s, there is a huge Spanish **influence** there. You can see it in the food and art, the building style and religion. The Spanish were Catholic, and most of Mexico is still Catholic today. Catholicism is a kind of **Christianity**.

Once we get to Mexico City, we are going to meet my friend Gabriel, who is 9 years old. He plays soccer for the team at his school. Gabriel has promised to show us some great surprises during our stay here. These include pyramids and butterfly forests. We'll also visit Aztec Stadium, the largest sports stadium in North America!

Right now, we'd better practice our Spanish. As soon as we get off this bus, we are embarking on a walking tour of the city. I don't know about you, but I'm ready! So let's go . . . or as they say here: *vamonos (Vah-moh-nos)*!

MEXICAN FLAG

The Mexican flag has bars of green, white, and red with a picture in the middle. This picture—or coat of arms—is an eagle on top of a prickly pear catcus devouring a snake. The cactus sits above water. Can you guess what this symbolizes? It represents the Aztec legend of the founding of Tenochtitlán (Teh-nohch-teet-LAN), the city built on top of a lake that is now Mexico City.

SPANISH 101

Here are some basic Spanish words and phrases for you to learn by yourself or with your friends!

SOCCER	FUTBAL [FOOHT-bohl]
HELLO	HOLA [OH–Lah]
GOODBYE	ADIOS [Ah-Dee-OHS]
FRIEND	AMIGO [Ah-MEE-Go]
SCHOOL	ESCUELA [Es-QUE-Lah]
BOOK	LIBRO [LEE-Broh]
MOTHER	MADRE [MAh-dre]
FATHER	PADRE [PAh-dre]
SISTER	HERMANA [Er-MAH-Nah]
BROTHER	HERMANO [Er-MAH-Noh]
GOOD MORNING	BUENOS DIAS [Boo-eh-nos-DEE-as]
GOOD NIGHT	BUENAS NOCHES [Boo-eh-nas-NO-ches]
COME PLAY	VEN A JUGAR [Ven-ah-HOO-gar]
I AM HUNGRY	TENGO HAMBRE [TENG-go-AHM-bray]
LET'S PLAY	JUGAMOS [Hoo-GAH-mohs]

SALSA SNACK

We will use some Mexican ingredients to make a simple avocado salsa. Have an adult help you with the chopping.

1 Chop up the avocado, tomato, and about one quarter of the red onion into small cubes. Add them to the bowl.

2 Tear the cilantro into little pieces, and add it to the other ingredients in the bowl.

3 Squeeze in some lime juice. Add some salt and pepper, a pinch of garlic powder, and a pinch of chili pepper flakes or sauce.

SUPPLIES

◊ chopping board
◊ knife
◊ bowl
◊ ripe avocado
◊ ripe tomato
◊ red onion
◊ cilantro
◊ lime
◊ salt and pepper
◊ garlic powder
◊ chili pepper flakes or sauce
◊ corn chips

FOOD FUN

Here are some famous foods that were discovered or used in ancient Mexico:

SQUASH	Calabaza [Ka-La-BAH-sah]
AVOCADO	Aguacate [Ah-Gawh-KAH-Teh]
CHOCOLATE	Chocolate [Cho-co-LAH-Teh]
CHILI PEPPERS	Chiles [CHee-Les]
TOMATOES	Jitomates [Hee-Toh-MAH-Tehs]
VANILLA	Vainilla [Vah-ee-NEE-Yah]
PAPAYA	Papaya [Pah-PAH-Yah]
JICAMA (HICK-ah-Mah)	Jícama [HEE-Kah-Mah]
TURKEY	Guajolote [Wah-ho-LO-Teh]
PEANUTS	Cacahuates [Kah-Kah-WHAH-tehs]
MAIZE (CORN)	Maíz [Mah-EES]

4 Mix the ingredients together to create your very own salsa, made with ingredients discovered in Mexico! Use the salsa as a dip for the chips and enjoy!

A TRIP BACK IN TIME

After sitting for so long, it feels great to get off the bus. As the door creaks open, I can see Gabriel waiting for me. Gabriel and I shake hands, and then hug. He tells me that when I meet his mother, she will give me the traditional Mexican greeting of one kiss on the cheek.

A Trip Back in Time

Gabriel has a surprise for me. Since today is Sunday, it's bike day in Mexico City. To cut down on pollution and encourage families to exercise, the city has closed some of the city streets to cars. Gabriel has brought a bike for each of us to ride!

I am hungry after my long trip. Our first stop is a delicious local food stand. We buy *nopales* (Noh-pah-Les), which are cactus pads with the needles taken off, and *flor de calabaza* (FLoR-deh-Kah-La-BAH-sah), fried squash blossoms. Mmm . . . tasty!

As we bike to our final destination, Alameda Square, there is so much to see and do. There are buildings from the 1500s all the way to the present day. We can actually see changes in style from city block to city block.

"Gabriel points out that our ride is almost like a trip back in time because we can observe so much of Mexico's history."

We stop at one of those buildings. It's a beautiful cathedral with massive arches. The Catedral Metropolitana is the largest church in all of North and South America. It is a work of art in itself.

MERCADO LOCAL

Local markets are found all across Mexico. *El Mercado* (EhL-mer-cah-doh) has fresh fruits and vegetables, as well as prepared food. Artists sell arts and crafts. It's an amazing sight! There are miniature papier-mâché figures, paintings on flattened pieces of tin, and hand-woven blankets and hats.

When we visit a candy stand in *El Mercado*, we encounter a swarm of bees! I am a little concerned, but Gabriel laughs at my worry. He says the bees tell us which candy is the sweetest. The buzz is a good sign!

Together, we pick up a few sweet treats, including a mango-flavored lollipop sprinkled with chili powder. The sweet and spicy taste seems strange at first but I like it!

DIEGO RIVERA

Diego Rivera was one of Mexico's most famous artists. He was known for his murals. These are paintings done on a wall or other large surface. At the Diego Rivera Museum, Gabriel and I look at one of his most well-known murals, "Dream of a Sunday Afternoon in Alameda Park."

Incredibly, it is Sunday afternoon, and we are headed exactly to that park! It is another reminder of the amazing connection between the past and present. You can see the actual mural at www.soccerworldadventure.com.

Our next stop is Alameda Park. All of Gabriel's pals are there to play a game of soccer! It's the perfect finish to my first day in Mexico, just kicking the soccer ball around and relaxing with my new friends.

BEE A LIGHT

Remember the bees that told us which candy was the sweetest? They also produce beeswax in their hives. We can use the beeswax to make candles! For this project, make sure you ask an adult for help.

SUPPLIES

◊ beeswax sheets, any color and scent, from a local store or the Internet
◊ scissors
◊ wick
◊ clean, flat work surface

1 Fold a beeswax sheet in half, very carefully. Cut the sheet in half along the fold line.

2 Place the half-sheet in front of you on your work surface.

3 Lay the wick across the bottom edge of the sheet. Cut the wick so that it hangs a half-inch past the beeswax on either end of the bottom edge.

Tuck the wick by rolling up the bottom edge of the sheet and sealing it over the wick. Make sure it is nice and tight all the way across.

 Now you can begin rolling your candle! Using both hands and applying even pressure, roll up the wax towards the top edge of the sheet. Go slowly and make sure you are rolling straight.

 When you get about 2 inches from the top, roll it as tight as you can, just like you did at the bottom when you put the wick in for the first time.

7 Turn the candle over. Using your fingertips, gently seal the top edge into the rest of the candle. Run your fingers across the whole edge so it becomes part of the candle. Don't push too hard, or you will crush the beeswax.

 Cut the wick even with the bottom of the candle. The wick at the top should stick out about ¼ inch. Your candle is done!

WORDS 2 KNOW

mariachi: traditional Mexican folk music played by a small group of musicians.

After playing soccer, Gabriel and I walk to Garibaldi Square. We pass a stand selling *agua fresca* (Ah-GOO-ah-fres-Kah), or fruit waters. There are all different kinds, and the vendor lets us try mashing some of the fresh fruit! We both get *agua de sandia* (Ah-GOO-ah-deh-Sahn-DEE-ah), which is watermelon, and find a bench to sit and cool down.

It's a beautiful evening and a local **mariachi** (Mah-ree-ah-CHEE) band begins to play. This gives me a chance to ask Gabriel about Mexican music. Most Americans are familiar with mariachi music in general. But he tells me that every region in Mexico has its own style.

After a little while, Gabriel heads home for dinner. Tomorrow we have an all-day adventure planned. He promises me it will be the trip of a lifetime.

MAGIC MEXICO

It's early morning when I pick up Gabriel and his parents at his house in Mexico City. It is wonderful to meet Paola and Diego. Sure enough, his mother kisses me on the cheek in the traditional Mexican greeting. I try to say good morning to them in Spanish, but mix up my phrases and say goodnight instead! Even though they laugh, I can tell they understand me.

Gabriel still won't tell me where we are going today. He wants it to be a surprise. The drive is beautiful, as the scenery changes from a big city to rolling fields to pine trees.

After three hours we arrive at Morelia (Moh-reh-lee-ah), a city filled with **colonial** and other historical buildings. I notice the ancient **channels** that carried water to the town hundreds of years ago.

CORUNDAS

Hungry for a snack, Gabriel and I order some *corundas* **(Koh-roon-Dahs) at a local food stand. These are cornhusk pouches filled with steamed corn meal. They are so delicious that I buy three more for the car trip.**

After driving past many small villages, we finally arrive at our destination and park the car. But we still have a long hike ahead of us, down into a **valley**. As we walk Gabriel tells me about what he wants to do when he grows up. He is interested in **environmental** issues and wants to make a difference in his **community**.

We pass a sign for "Santuario de Mariposas El Rosario" (San-too-ah-ree-oh-deh-Mah-ree-poh-sah-Ehl-Roh-sah-ree-oh). Gabriel smiles and tells me to wait for the translation.

Suddenly, we come to the most amazing view I have ever seen. I am so stunned that I cannot find words in Spanish or English to describe it.

"There, in front of us, is a forest full of butterflies!"

I remember that the Spanish word for butterfly is "Mariposa," like on the sign. Thousands of black-and-orange butterflies cover the pine and fir trees. There are so many that the forest looks like it's in constant motion. Their wings are like fluttering leaves in the wind. The butterflies have come to rest on their annual **migration** from Canada.

WORDS 2 KNOW

colonial: relating to the time when people from Spain settled in Mexico, and the area was a colony of Spain.

channels: ditches directing water from a stream or river.

valley: a low area of land between mountains.

environmental: having to do with the environment.

community: a group of people with something in common.

migration: moving from one place to another every year.

WORDS 2 KNOW

natural wonder: something amazing in the natural world.

serenade: sing to someone.

We stay for hours, taking in the beauty of this **natural wonder**. I know that I will never forget this experience. I take a picture and label it "Magic Mariposa."

We are so tired when we return to Mexico City that we relax there with Gabriel's family. After a few days, we head to the floating gardens of Xochimilco (So-Chee-MIL-Koh). These gardens used to provide food for the ancient city of Tenochtitlán.

This was a city with canals and waterways instead of streets. The Aztecs created "floating" islands out of reeds and muck and dirt, held to the lake floor by planted tree roots. They grew food on these unique gardens.

Today, we rent a brightly painted boat, called a *trajinera* (Trah-HEE-neh-rah). Each boat has its own name.

"It's like a floating mall, except they come to you with food, music, clothing, flowers, and gifts."

The driver uses a longstick to push the boat. Other boats float by, offering food and other items to buy. Some carry musicians on board, who **serenade** us with great Mexican music.

As we float along, Gabriel points to the new project on the banks of the canal. People are composting, and harvesting the algae from the water to feed the soil. Composting takes anything that was once alive, like old fruits and vegetables, and puts it back into the soil to make it richer for plants to grow.

SEMBRADORES URBANOS

Sembradores Urbanos (Sehm-Brah-doh-res-OOr-bah-nos) is one of many projects in Mexico dedicated to helping the environment. Meaning Urban Planters, this organization runs city gardens. It teaches kids and adults about composting and growing vegetables in small spaces.

The boat trip sure is relaxing. Gabriel tells me it's good we are off our feet. Tomorrow we will be doing lots of walking on another special trip. I can't imagine anything more special than today.

COMPOST CHALLENGE

Composting takes waste fruit, vegetables, and plants and changes them into a rich soil for plants. You can set up a compost bin in your backyard or at school.

1 Pick a place for your bin. Either use a container for your bin or make your own by bending a short length of chicken wire fence into a U shape.

2 Put a 6-inch layer of dead material at the bottom of the bin. This material is rich in **carbon**. Add a 6-inch layer of live material. This is high in **nitrogen**.

SUPPLIES

◊ container or short length of chicken wire fence
◊ dead material: brown leaves, dried pine needles, shredded newspaper, sawdust
◊ live material: old fruits and vegetables, still-green weeds and grass clippings
◊ shovel
◊ soil
◊ water source

3 Add a shovelful of soil to the mix. Soil contains **microorganisms**, insects, and worms that will break everything down. Water the soil layer.

 4 Repeat Steps 2 and 3 until the bin is full. Now you just need to wait a few weeks!

5 You will know when the compost is ready because it will turn a rich, deep brown, and smell earthy. After this happens, spread your compost around the bases of the plants that you already have, or put it at the bottoms of the holes you dig for new plants. The compost helps feed the plants!

 6 Plant some of the Mexican vegetables that we talked about earlier, such as chili peppers or tomatoes, and use the compost to help them grow.

WORDS 2 KNOW

carbon: an element found in all living things.

nitrogen: the most common element in the earth's atmosphere.

element: a pure substance such as gold or oxygen that cannot be broken down into something simpler.

microorganism: a living thing that is so small you can only see it with a microscope. Bacteria is a microorganism that breaks down dead material.

THE PAST IS THE PRESENT

Today, Gabriel and his family come to meet me at my hotel in the morning. They ask me if I am ready for a very long trip. Where are we going? Gabriel grins and tells me, "We're traveling back in time 2,000 years. Apparently, we are visiting some of Mexico's most famous *ancient* sites.

Our first stop is the amazing ruins of Teotihuacán (Teh-oh-tee-WAH-kan) just outside Mexico City. I thought **pyramids** existed only in Egypt. But here, right in front of us, is the incredible Pyramid of the Sun. It's the third-largest pyramid in the world.

"To reach the top, we will have to climb 242 giant steps!"

WORDS 2 KNOW

ancient: very old, from the distant past.

pyramid: a monument in the shape of a triangle with a square base.

winded: out of breath.

Gabriel challenges me to a race, and soon we are running up the steps as quickly as we can. Panting, I yell out *"Rapido!"* (Rah-pee-doh), which means "fast" in Spanish. Gabriel and I finish in an exact tie! The altitude leaves me **winded**, so I catch my breath and take in the majestic view.

TEOTIHUACÁN

Teotihuacán was the main city of the Aztecs. At the height of its glory, it may have housed over 100,000 people. There are many ideas about why it eventually disappeared. Overuse of the land may have ruined the soil so the Aztecs could not grow enough food.

Below us are dozens of **temples**. The Avenue of the Dead connects them, runnning from the Pyramid of the Moon past the Pyramid of the Sun. As we take in the view, I think about what life must have been like for the people who once lived here.

After lunch, we all walk down the Avenue of the Dead to the Temple of the Plumed Serpent, or Templo de Quetzacoatl (keh-tsa-KO-atl). Quetzacoatl is a feathered, snake-like god.

"There are paintings and carvings of Quetzacoatl everywhere."

WORDS 2 KNOW

temple: a building used as a place to worship.

obsidian: black volcanic glass formed by the rapid cooling of lava.

mine: an underground area where valuable rocks are dug up.

trade: to exchange one thing for something else.

Some of the carvings have eyes made out of **obsidian**, a shiny black rock. "As I move around the temple, the eyes seem to follow me!"

I have never seen obsidian before. Gabriel informs me that the whole city of Teotihuacán was founded on an obsidian **mine**.

"People used obsidian to trade for the things they needed, just like we use coins and dollar bills."

We end our day at the Observatorio (Ob-ser-vah-toh-ree-oh). This man-made cave has a hole in the ceiling so you can see the night sky through it. It gives me the chills to realize that, hundreds of years ago, people used to come down here and watch the stars, just like we're doing now.

Later that week, we fly to the Yucatán (yoo-kah-TAN) where we visit the Maya ruins of Chichén Itzá (Chee-chen-EET-zah). Remember, the Maya were great mathematicians and invented a number system that was one of the first to use a zero. Chichén Itzá is as amazing as Teotihuacán, with massive temples and beautiful carvings.

"Some of these famous pyramids are over 1,500 years old!"

ROCK YOUR WORLD

Rocks are divided into categories by the way they formed.

Igneous Rocks form when liquid rock cools. This liquid rock is called magma when it lies under the earth's surface. It is lava when it flows out onto the surface from volcanoes. *Obsidian* is an igneous rock.

Sedimentary Rocks are made of materials like sand, mud, pebbles, or shells pressed together over time. *Sandstone* is a sedimentary rock.

Metamorphic Rocks are igneous or sedimentary rocks that transform over thousands of years from high heat or pressure. *Marble* is a metamorphic rock.

I think Gabriel must be joking when he asks me if I would like to play a game of soccer here. It's hard to believe that the ancient Maya had a soccer field. However, Gabriel grins in triumph when we arrive at the Juego de Pelota (peh-LOH-tah).

This was the court of an ancient Maya game similar to soccer. Players used their hips, thighs, and knees to juggle a ball and send it through a high hoop. I wish we had a *pelota*, or ball, so we could try it.

Gabriel wants to give me a clue about where we are headed next and runs all the way to the opposite end of the court. My mouth drops open in shock when Gabriel starts talking. It sounds like he is standing right next to me. Gabriel takes advantage of the incredible way sound carries in the Juego de Pelota to tell me, "I hope you are ready to get soaked!"

"I hope you are ready to get soaked!"

CURRENT CURRENCY

Create your own currency system with your friends or classmates, just like the Maya did! Do you know how our money system has different coins that represent different values? They are all coins but their shapes and design represent a value of money. Think about items you have around your house that you can use for your money system.

 Place all your items in front of you, and then decide what each one will be worth in your money system. For example, if you are using different fruits and vegetables, then maybe each raisin is worth a dime and 10 raisins makes a dollar. One carrot represents a dollar. One apple equals ten dollars.

2 Once everyone in your group knows what each item is worth, then you can go ahead and start trading. You might sell your favorite hat to your friend for 8 carrots, or buy a piece of gum for 3 raisins!

3 Ask an adult how much various items in your house, such as groceries, clothing, and toys, cost. Figure out what each item is worth in your money system. If your new jacket cost $45.90, that would be 4 apples, 5 carrots, and 9 raisins in our money system above.

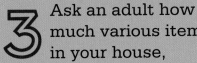

SUPPLIES

Any of the following:
◊ different-colored buttons
◊ different pieces of cereal
◊ different fruits and vegetables
◊ different types of school supplies, such as pencils, pens, and erasers

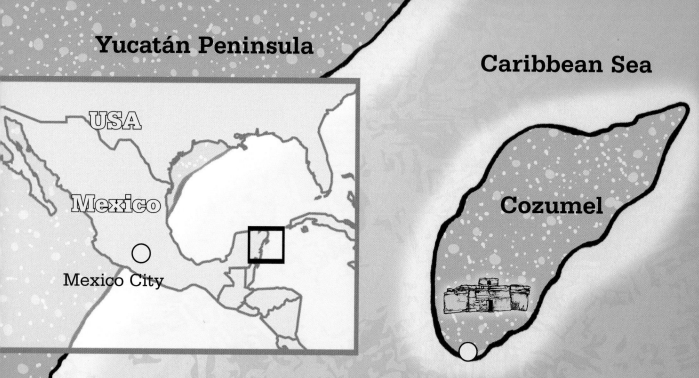

Yucatán Peninsula

Caribbean Sea

USA

Mexico

Mexico City

Cozumel

Parque Punta Sur

WATER WORLD

We're off to explore one of Mexico's many *coastal* cultures. Gabriel is taking me to the Mayan Riviera, in the southeast corner of Mexico, along the Caribbean Sea. Our first stop is the island of Cozumel. Cozumel is famous for its clear, blue-green waters. It is one of the best diving and snorkeling spots in the entire world.

Water World

We begin at Parque Punta Sur (PAR-keh-poon-tah-soor). This is a **national preserve** for animals and birds. As Gabriel and I walk to an ancient Maya lighthouse here, he tells me that it carries a cool surprise. When the wind blows in a certain direction, the lighthouse makes a whistling sound!

From the lighthouse, we can see a real-life crocodile lagoon and the island's spectacular beaches and surrounding water. We head down to the beach to take our first snorkeling trip.

"I can't wait any longer to dive into the ocean!"

We rent masks, snorkels, and fins, and swim out to the **reef**. Floating on the surface and looking down into the water below, we see schools of brightly colored fish.

coastal: land by the sea.

national preserve: an area of land protected from human activities like hunting and building because it is so beautiful and special.

reef: ridge of coral or rock near the water's surface.

34

Suddenly, I feel something swim up next to me and I shrink back in surprise. Is it a shark? No—just a harmless manta ray, gliding along and checking us out!

I wish that Gabriel and I could go **scuba diving**, because I love the freedom of swimming underwater. You can move in any direction, even up or down. To me, it's the closest thing to flying that you can get here on Earth. Diving is my favorite activity . . . after soccer, of course.

"Maybe in the future I'll combine both of my passions, and invent an underwater soccer game!"

The next day, Gabriel and I leave Cozumel to visit Aktun Chen (ak-TOON-chen) on the mainland. This collection of underwater **caves** is almost 5 million years old!

WORDS 2 KNOW

scuba diving: swimming under water with a container of air connected to a mouthpiece.

cave: large, hollowed out space underground.

minerals: substances in rocks.

oxygen: gas that animals need to breathe.

current: steady flow of water in a certain direction.

CAVE OF THE SLEEPING SHARKS

In an underwater cave off the coast of Cancún, there are sharks that appear to nap or doze on the bottom. This seems impossible, because sharks need to keep moving in order to breathe. They must have water constantly flowing over their gills to take in **oxygen**. Scientists believe they may be able to stay still because of the strength of the **current** in the cave. The current moves water over the sharks' gills for them, so they can take a break from swimming!

Aktun Chen is like an entire underground city of caves. There are giant rooms filled with stone icicles, called

stalactites and stalagmites. They hang from the ceiling or rise up from the floor.

These structures are formed out of **minerals** left behind by water many years ago. Standing here below the surface of the earth, I feel like I am on another planet.

Early the next morning, Gabriel and I head to Hidden Worlds Cenote Park. After a long ride through the jungle we snorkel in caves with incredible underground pools of transparent green water. The cool

CENOTE

A cenote is a sinkhole, or a place where the earth collapses in on itself. It fills with groundwater. This is the water that runs below the earth's surface.

water is so clear that we can see all the way to the bottom. We can also see the sky above through the cave's natural skylight.

Tomorrow in Mexico City we will check out Mexico's soccer scene. But on our way back home, we stop at a beach birthday celebration. The family invites us to join them! We eat from a whole fish, and even get to hit the piñata. This one is filled with oranges, sugar cane, peanuts, and a special candy called *Colacion* (Koh-la-Cee-ohn). As the sun sets, we play soccer on the sand with the kids. Now that's what I call awesome!

37

WATER MAGIC

In nature, rainwater seeps through rocks in the ground, a process that helps clean it. Here is a fun experiment to show exactly how this process works. The sand and charcoal trap the particles of dirt in the water, making it cleaner!

SUPPLIES

◊ paper coffee filter
◊ funnel
◊ charcoal gravel from a gardening shop or pet store
◊ sand
◊ empty container
◊ container full of muddy water

1 Place the coffee filter in the funnel. Put a layer of charcoal at the bottom of the coffee filter.

2 Add a layer of sand on top of the charcoal. Place the funnel over the empty container.

3 While someone else pours the muddy water into the funnel, look at the water as it comes out the bottom. Is it clearer?

SPORTS SI!

Our trip to Mexico has to include my favorite sport, soccer. It's a huge sport here. What better place to watch a match than Aztec Stadium? It's the largest sports stadium in North America. It can hold over 100,000 people, and has been the site of not one, but two, FIFA World Cup Finals. Gabriel tells me that the stadium hosts many different teams and games.

The Mexican national team, nicknamed El Tri (Ehl-tr-ee), plays here. El Tri means three colors. The team is called that because Mexico has three colors in its flag: green, red, and white.

Today, there is a match between Club America, the stadium's popular home team, and Cruz Azul (Croos-Ah-zool). These teams play in the Primera División de Mexico (Pree-meh-rah-dee-vee-zee-ohn), the top level of competition here. In the United States, we have different leagues for baseball: A, AA, AAA, and the top-rated Major League Baseball. The same is true of soccer in Mexico.

"I love being part of such a loud and excited crowd."

While we cheer on the players, Gabriel tells me there is another version of soccer played in Mexico, called futsal. It is played mostly indoors.

FIFA

The FIFA World Cup is a soccer tournament that takes place every four years with the national teams from countries all over the world. FIFA stands for the Fédération Internationale de Football Association. It's like the government of world soccer. The name is in the French language.

40

The court surface has no walls or boards, and the ball is smaller than a regular soccer ball, with less bounce.

I ask about other sports in Mexico. Gabriel jokes that I may have heard about another game played along the border, called baseball. He also says that there is one more sport that he would like me to see before our trip ends . . . Lucha Libre wrestling!

Tomorrow, we will say goodbye. Until then, we are determined to have a wonderful time, and we enjoy every second of the match.

LUCHA LIBRE

Lucha Libre (Loo-chah-LEE-BREH) wrestling started in Mexico a hundred years ago, when wrestlers started to wear masks and costumes. The wrestlers played good and evil characters as they fought. The "good guys" became huge stars, with movies and comic books modeled after them. Gabriel has the perfect character for me, "The Soccer Dog," because one of my nicknames is E-Dog.

SAYING GOODBYE

T he time has come to say goodbye to Gabriel. I thank him for the amazing trip, and for showing me the wonders of Mexico—pyramids and underwater caves, butterflies and beaches. I especially loved the exciting soccer match. It has been a special adventure.

In *Soccer World*, we always exchange gifts at the end of the trip. Gabriel gives me a small papier-mâché skull with my name painted across the forehead. At first, I am a little frightened by the gift. However, Gabriel tells me that it is associated with the Day of the Dead, an important Mexican holiday. During this holiday Mexicans celebrate the fact that they are alive.

"Truly, this is a gift that honors life."

I give Gabriel a South African bracelet from our first *Soccer World* adventure. Each person we visit gets something from the place we visited before. My second gift is a *Soccer World* mini-soccer ball. I hope Gabriel will take it with him wherever he goes and send me pictures.

WHERE NEXT?

Where do you think we should go on our next soccer adventure? Email me to share your ideas.

MAKE A DIFFERENCE

Gabriel gives back by helping the environment. You can give back too. Use the Internet or library to find a project to support. Maybe it's replanting forests or saving sea turtles or helping to rebuild poor communities.

Create a poster or a video to spread awareness about your cause. Do a report. Write letters to your friends about the organization. Or ask your parents if you can do some fundraising. Have a bake sale, sell hand-drawn T-shirts or homemade bracelets, or run a lemonade stand. Get creative and have a fun event for everyone. What matters is that you help Gabriel make Mexico a better place to live. Email me at Ethan@soccerworldadventure.com and tell me all about it!

GLOSSARY

altitude: height above sea level.

ancient: very old, from the distant past.

astronomy: the study of the stars and planets.

border: where one country meets another.

carbon: an element found in all living things.

cave: large, hollowed out space underground.

channels: ditches directing water from a stream or river.

Christianity: a religion whose followers believe in Jesus Christ.

coastal: land by the sea.

colonial: the time when people from Spain settled in Mexico, and it was a colony of Spain.

community: a group of people with something in common.

conqueror: the winner in a war.

consequence: a result of something happening.

culture: a way of life of a group of people.

current: steady flow of water in a certain direction.

eclipse: when the moon moves between the sun and the earth, blocking the sun's light.

element: a pure substance such as gold or oxygen that cannot be broken down into something simpler.

environment: the natural world around us including plants, animals, and air.

environmental: having to do with the environment.

influence: have an effect on someone or something.

mariachi: traditional Mexican folk music played by a small group of musicians.

microorganism: a living thing so small you can only see it with a microscope.

migration: moving from one place to another every year.

mine: an underground area where valuable rocks are dug up.

minerals: substances in rocks.

national preserve: land protected from human activities because it is so beautiful and special.

natural wonder: something amazing in the natural world.

Glossary & Index

nitrogen: the most common element in the earth's atmosphere.

obsidian: black volcanic glass formed by the rapid cooling of lava.

oxygen: gas that animals need to breathe.

pollution: waste that harms the environment.

pyramid: a monument in the shape of a triangle with a square base.

reef: ridge of coral or rock near the water's surface.

scuba diving: swimming under water with a container of air connected to a mouthpiece.

serenade: sing to someone.

temple: a building used as a place to worship.

trade: to exchange one thing for something else.

valley: a low area of land between mountains.

winded: out of breath.